MORE CHOIR PRAYERS

In memory of Marie Hunt,
who was a woman of prayerful song.

More Choir  Prayers

Jeanne Hunt

PASTORAL PRESS
PORTLAND · OREGON

ISBN: 0-912405-67-8

CONTENTS

INTRODUCTION

An axiom of our contemporary renewal of worship is that liturgy is first and foremost prayer. Prayer is evoked and sustained by any number of factors: suitable environment, a sense of reverence, attention to ritual detail, and the like. But the most important element here might be that those ministering to a people at worship themselves be prayerful servants. This includes not only the presiding minister and various auxiliary ministers, but also the members of the choir, namely, those members of the assembly who are called upon to lead and enhance the sung prayer of the gathered people.

Over the past few years this understanding has taken root among ever so many choirs, whose members are now accustomed to praying together during their weekly rehearsals. When *Choir Prayers* was first published in 1986, I intended to share my own efforts, born out of personal experience as a choir member, at formulating formulas of thanksgiving, praise, and petition that others might use, with or without adaptations. Some choirs have been stimulated to create their own texts. The success of the first volume prompted Pastoral Press to request more such prayers. In addition to models for use during particular seasons and times of the year, included here are many texts of a more general nature, suitable for ordinary time.

Admittedly, these prayers are not in the classic western tradition of prayer formulas. Being more akin to the compositions of Michael Quoist, which were so popular in the years immediately following Vatican II, they are reflective texts often springing out of situations known so well by choir members. And this, I venture, is how most of us singers pray at those informal moments when we need to focus or refocus our musical endeavors. We speak in simple terms, concretely, without rhetoric, and yet in such a way that our experiences unfold for us what it means to be servants ... of God, of people at worship, and of the art of music.

Beginning the Choir Year

Bless Us in Our Beginnings

*L*ord, tonight we take our seats again,
and we begin to sing.
We are well rested.
Summer was filled with freedom and fun,
    freedom to worship whenever we wished on
    Sunday morning,
    freedom to spend evenings
    for our own pleasure,
    no meetings ... no rehearsals.
Just the good, sweet rest that summer is all about.

But now it is over.
We return.
We know full well what we are in for, Lord.
Getting up from the supper table
    and going out the door,
    when we'd rather keep sitting.
Working up the mental energy
    to concentrate on new music,
    when we'd rather unwind
    in front of the television.
So, why do we come, Lord?
It would be so easy to let someone else
    be part of the choir.
In the end, it is simple.

We are here because of a love of God,
      a love of his people,
      a love of music.
It is a love that far surpasses the urge
      to choose an easier way.
Lord, you have gifted us,
      called us to do your work
      in this vineyard of song.
We have heard your invitation and have
      responded.

Bless us in our beginnings, Lord.
Give us the fortitude to remain faithful
      to your call.
Help us to serve well.

Singing a New Song

*L*ord, joining a choir is intimidating.
    Twenty or more pieces of music
    we have never seen before, others,
    some more difficult than others,
    but each making us wonder,
    what we are doing here
The rest of the choir sings with ease,
    full, confident voices,
    while we approach each note with strange
    reserve.
Will we ever be able to sing with their
    confidence?

Lord, help us to remember
    that everyone began in the same manner.
Confidence came slowly,
    after much work and commitment.
Lord, you never give wine
    without labor in the vineyard first.
Help us trust you in this decision to sing here,
    trust in ourselves that with your help
    and our hard work
    this venture will be all we had hoped for.
Beginning is never easy.
It always takes trust.

So, Lord, tonight we pray for each other,
   especially those to whom all our music
   is new.
Give them patience, make them
   long-suffering,
      even if they must do more listening than
      singing in the beginning.
In the end, make our music their music.
Make our "joyful noise" more beautiful
   by their coming.

Advent and
Christmas

An Advent Prayer

*I*n night's quiet,
   when we have time and silence to think,
   the songs of this season
   come drifting into our minds.
In the quiet they are welcomed,
   and our spirits somehow delight
   in this sweet Advent time.
The dark seems comfortable,
   and our songs fit the mood of night.
"Come, long awaited Savior,"
   into the darkness of our lives.
There is a lot of darkness in our lives …
   so many places where we live without God.
It is not easy to stay with him.
It is not always easy to find him
   in our work, in traffic, in our families.
But now, gathered together,
   we come to his light.
We can feel the warmth of his love.
We can sing about his coming.
Here we can find this Jesus the Christ
   who is willing to walk in our
   darkness with us,
   born to become our light.

Lord, grace us with hope as we sing tonight ...
 hope in the kingdom your share,
 hope in the way you always care for us,
 hope in our song and the miracle it brings.

What We Sow in Tears, We Reap in Rejoicing

*L*ord, these Advent days call us to remember
  the somber notes of our lives,
    the moments when there was
    only darkness,
    days that we cannot recall living ...
    days when there was nothing left
    but emptiness.
We cried out through our tears.
Advent moment of life
    when we could not save ourselves.

In that painful silence
    a solitary, sweet note begins.
Sometimes sung by a prophet,
    more often sung by your own voice.
The voice in the wilderness.
The voice of God, Emmanuel,
    stirs the stilled heart.
    Some small glimpse of hope is intoned.
We hear a note and choose to respond.
A harmony begins.
The dark of night becomes a prelude
    to rejoicing.

Out of our depths
    Christ sings his salvation song.
We are, somehow, reborn.
Lord, our Advent song is richer
    for our suffering,
    for we sing from our hearts.
We tenderly proclaim the Savior,
    a Savior who is born to each of us
    not just once,
    in time long ago,
    but in the multitude of Advent moments
    we carry in our hearts that compel us
    to sing
    "Come, long awaited Savior."

Wind Song at Christmas

*L*ord, the world is quieting into
  Christmas peace.
Our hearts await the feast.
Snow surrounds the earth
    as if this blanket of white
    promises the gift within.
We come to these final rehearsals
    well prepared.
It is good to be comfortable with our music.
It allows your spirit to enter the sound.
Spirit song is such a gift, Lord.
It only comes when we trust enough,
    relax enough,
    to sing with inspiration.
A sound apart,
    something beyond our skill occurs.
Thank you, Lord, for these weeks
    of preparation.
Now allow us to sing in your spirit
    so that our hymns might make Christmas
    in the hearts of your people.
May our music be the wind song of grace,
    wind song bringing Christmas joy …
    Christmas love …
    Christmas peace.
Wind song born of the spirit
    in this quieting before the feast.

Christmas Night

*L*ord, tonight we lose ourselves
   in the infant,
    tiny, vulnerable, new-born,
    whom we encounter as the savior of the
    world.
We have come to this night with our gift
   of music.
It is the finest we have,
    well polished, glimmering,
    sparkling winter song,
    meant for infant ears as the first song of his
    birthing night.
Help us to find you in our worship tonight.
Let our music take us to a more tender place.
Lift our souls to your birthing place,
    where all creation pauses in awe
    at the possibility, the reality of communion,
    the blending of our humanity and your
    divinity.
May the rapture of the miracle enfold us,
    inspire us,
    so that all may be filled
    with Christmas holiness.

Dazzle Us, Lord

*L*ord, the songs of Christmas are fading.
　Our minds and hearts no longer hum
　　those sweet lullabies of birth.
We begin to look for some new direction
　　for our inspiration.
Singers need to be inspired …
　　a feast … a challenging work …
　　a celebration …
　　anything to budge us from the doldrums
　　of deep winter.
The earth is sleeping in browns, grays, and
　　white,
　　and so too our spirits.
Lord, splash us with some musical color.
Dazzle us with unexpected harmony.
Surprise us with a new work.
Overwhelm us with a spectrum of radiant
　　sound,
　　a prism of translucent musical color.
Help us to rise above the apathy
　　of this winter gray.
Fill our hearts with hope and excitement.
Pour out the energy,
　　the excitement,
　　the inspiration
　　that make music alive.

We are here to bring a taste of heaven
through our sound,
a heaven radiant with musical color,
magnificent,
dazzling,
marvelous,
supernatural,
in winter's bleakness.

January's Song

Lord, it is January.
   Nights are very long,
   and the earth is blanketed in a gray mist.
The sweet sounds of the Savior's birth fade,
   and we are left with the remnant
   of the feast.
Like the discarded evergreens awaiting the
   trash,
   so too are our spirits.
Life quiets into a sleep now,
   and we are forced to dream dreams about
   the warmth of the sun,
   the color of a burgundy rose,
   the smell of newly turned earth.
Dreaming is the gift of January,
   and only those who have danced to
   the song of dreams
   can love this time.
It is a time to spend
   with what might be possible.
In this quiet, Lord,
   you speak to those who dream.
You speak about your dreams for us.
And because there is nothing to distract us,
   we hear.

Could it be, Lord, that the real gift of
    Christmas
    is the grace, the hope,
    that enable us to dream?
Is the nativity the call to believe
    in something beyond us?
To believe in mustard seeds becoming
    mountains ...
    to believe in walking on water ...
    or the blind watching the sun rise.
Could it be that the dream songs of January
    are the gift, the vision of things to be?
Because the Savior dared to be born,
    and we dare to believe in your dream.

Lent
Easter
Pentecost

Lent Begins

*L*ord, we enter the season of Lent.
Adagio marks the beginning of our music.
Composers instruct us to sing with somber
  slowing.
We are enveloped in music's deeper velvet
  shades.
The mood is sobering, and we are called to
    put aside the joys of redemptive living
    and return to the dark moments of
    humankind.
That is not any easy thing to do, Lord.
We are kind of a "put your sunny side up"
  people.
Depression is not our strong suit.
We are living in the wonderful state
    of having heard the good news,
    news that radically changes the lives
    of all who have encountered
    the living Christ.
To affirm the light
    we must meet the darkness again.
To sing Alleluia with any conviction
    we must understand how to sing *Kyrie*.
So we willingly turn to this darkness.

We remember the pain, the sorrow,
    the burdens we have carried.
Each member of this choir could tell of
    the heartache
    that rests silently behind an easy smile.
So, Lord, it is your Son who invites us
    to sing of suffering and pain …
    to sing of mercy …
    to sing of all we have been saved from,
    to sing of a moment when one among us
    walked to his death for love.

Singing Tears

*L*ord, our ministry in these days of Lent is
    to translate the church's tears
  into music.
We are called to introspection,
    a quieting in the desert,
      where tears can flow like a living spring
      and cleanse us once again of our sins.
But, Lord, we have become callous to sin,
    hardened to evil,
      so that the tears do not come easily,
      and we excuse ourselves so willingly.
Music has the power to soften the hardest
    heart.
The songs of sorrow carry a grace,
    a grace that can touch our spirits
    and transport us to the desert places
    where the tears of decades might flow
    again.
And the miracle of healing and redemption
    happen to even the most lost among us.
Yet singing the songs of Lent takes care.
Sung with apathy they become a dirge
      that will fall lifeless
    and only reinforce the hardened heart.
Give our music depth of pathos.

Let the tender mercy of the cross
    flow in our somber tempo.
Ring our harmonies through with subtle
    darkness
    that bespeaks our dying Savior, Jesus.
Call us, the singers, into the presence
    of the Christ of the cross.
Let us sing with our own tears.
May our song be the sound of penance,
    our voices the cry of the chosen, the saved.

Nobody Knows the Trouble We Sing

*L*ord, Lent can weigh us down.
 Week after week, singing the liturgical
 blues eventually gets to us.
We have been singing four weeks of sweet
 sorrow in various slow and slower tempos.
We yearn for that first Easter Alleluia,
 for even a glimpse of the word *allegro*
 on a piece of music.
The Negro spiritual about nobody knowing
 the trouble we've seen
 is our present theme song.
For weeks we have sung of every spiritual
 trouble imaginable,
 and we are more than ready for a little
 musical joy.

Lord, teach us to encounter these Lenten
 hymns with your vision.
May we enter into a true spiritual longing
 for redemption,
 a redemption that is always occurring in
 our lives,
 not just one sad Friday centuries ago.
Help us find the beauty in these hymns
 of mercy and salvation.

The spirit of Lent comes to us from
    generations of expectation, an expectation
    realized only in Jesus and his cross.

We live in a time when things happen
    quickly …
    fast food, instant replay, quick dry …
    and you ask us to wait on your time
    to live out forty days of Lent
    without impatience.
We would prefer a "ten-day trial period,"
    then on to Easter, as is the custom in
    our high-tech, fast-lane world.
But you know a different pace,
    where weeks of Lent make Easter
    the reward of a patient heart.
Lord, as we continue with our Lenten days,
    keep us content with our slower tempo.
May we relish the journey to Calvary,
    and be willing to sing about it,
    willing to hear the words of repentance,
    willing to wait for the empty tomb.

Easter Light

Lord, thank you for our Easter sound.
Easter comes like the quiet dawn
   at the end of Lent's long night,
Sweet, unmistakable,
      morning light
      song.
With the first intoning words,
"Christ is our light,"
      so ancient, yet ever new,
      our hearts leap with expectation,
      expectation of new music,
      Alleluias,
      triumphant joy.
Lord, these sweet beginnings
      always amaze and delight.
A wordless wonder song provokes the mystery
      in us.
The moment of Easter is real.
The night that brings forth our song
      has a grace,
      a grace that changes what we sing.
The songs we practiced for weeks
      become finely polished works of art,
      works that cannot have life till that moment
      of Easter light.

Suddenly, through no power of our own, the songs
    come to life.

Life comes to music through the
    prayer-heart of the singer.
Black and white paper lies still,
    meaningless,
        till we singers leap into the grace of
        Easter light,
        and then the hymns take on vibrant life.
Lord, we thank you for that magic dawn
    when Christ surpassed death
    and brought an impossible rebirth.
Rebirth to every moment, every song,
    every breath.
It is gift.
It is mystery.
It is the beginning of heaven.
Alleluia.

Under the Spout
Where the Glory Comes Out

*L*ord, there's an old Pentecostal
   hymn than begins,
   "You're under the spout where the glory
   comes out."
Who are these people who sing about getting
   under a spout?
Spout time is rare in the church,
   but we caught a few drops this Easter.

The triumphant sound of brass,
   the singing of the *Exsultet*,
   brought the glory of Jesus Christ
   to full array.
We knew it,
   felt it,
   could almost see it.
We did, through your grace,
   what every choir is called to do.
   "Magnify the Lord in this place.
Make him larger than life
   through the miracle of song."
The church was alive with your glory,
   radiant with sun-tones of divine glory.

Orange, white, gold sounds ...
     the people looked overwhelmed, amazed ...
     no less than the women at the tomb.
So Lord, thank you
     for turning on the spout,
     for our moment in the glory stream.
It was edifying and inspiring.
This Easter we were under the spout
     where the glory comes out.

Shepherd Us, Lord

*L*ord, the post-Easter spring fever let-down
is upon us.
It is so easy to get discouraged, distracted,
and preoccupied as the weather warms,
and the music of spring seems so lovely.
But we cannot afford a mental vacation,
although we could really use one.
Tonight, Lord, our prayer is for
a renewed sense of fortitude,
and energy, an excitement.
Transform our lagging spirits.
Bring to these rows a new vitality
that will make the demands of what we are
doing less strenuous.
Let all this come easily, Lord.
Keep us going, for nothing worth doing
can be done without effort.
Bless our work.
Ease our burden.
Shepherd us, Lord.

Throughout the
Year

You Are the Salt of the Earth

"*Y*ou are the salt of the earth. What
    happens when salt goes flat?"
What happens when the choir
    as the salt of the liturgy goes flat?
Lord, going flat just seems to happen
    sometimes.
We may blame it on the weather,
    the day of the week,
    the tempo,
    anything that might relieve us of
    the burden.
But singers go flat because they are not being
    careful about breathing, volume,
    projection from the diaphram.
They get lazy and casual,
    and find themselves hopelessly lost.
Lord, spiritual salt and musical salt are really
    similar.
You call us to guard the moments of our day
    just as we do the moments of song.
To keep our salt tangy we must talk to you
    often in prayer.
We must always take time to notice the beauty
    around us,
    to listen to the burdens of another.
Salt is a precious gift.

You want a spicy, vibrant church bringing
    fire and joy to this tired planet.
And so it is with our song.
Give us the grace to keep it salty,
    bringing fire and life to your people.

Bless the Music Makers

*L*ord, this evening we hold in our hands
  twenty or more pieces of music.
So varied in their style,
    so diverse in their response to you,
    that we cannot help but wonder
    at this phenomenon of creativity.
What a gift it is to bring such a variance of
    musical prayer,
    to hear within the mind an unheard
    melody,
    to see the birth of that new song,
    coming out of our dialogue with God.
New notes, new prayer, new grace!
One composer finds expression in a gentle
    lyric style.
Another brings joy to life in an upbeat *allegro*.
Still another praises God in the beauty
    of classical sound.
And we are enriched by their sharing.
For it is not just paper we hold in our
    hands tonight.
We hold the workings of those who gave away
    a part of themselves
    to untold hundreds who sing their song.
We hold a treasure without price,

the treasure of a moment of inspiration,
when a music maker reached to us and
God,
and gave away a melody in common love.
Lord, help us remember to revere music
as a gift,
to sing each prayer as our own prayer.
For in a special way we do own this music.
We are the reed through which the
composer blows
the wind of song,
a wind that comes from you and is returned
to you by simple singers,
holders of a priceless treasure that lies
so quietly in our hands.

Bless the composers of this music.
Bless the singers of their notes.
Bless those who share it.

Be Ye Imitators of Christ

*L*ord, singing a fugue brings us into focus.
The rigid form, ordered for ages,
   comes to life in the composer's hands.
One voice introducing a theme,
   others following in marvelous variation.
A many splendored polyphony of sound.
Yet, with sureness the theme is sustained,
   each voice, given its moment to shine.
The lyric sopranos introduce the timeless
   theme,
      followed by the rich, velvet sound of
      the altos.
Tenors enter and the song soars to the heights
   like eagle's wings.
The thundering sound of the bass voice
   gives completion and fullness to our fugue.

Lord, the way of discipleship is like our fugue.
The life of your Son is the perfect theme,
   given for our salvation.
As we live in your ways we find inner harmony
   in imitation of Christ.
You have sung the first notes.
We follow in our unique variation.

Yet the form remains,
   brought to eternal and ever-changing
   life by your Spirit.
Your song is still being sung
   by those with the courage to
   imitate it.
Give us that courage, Lord,
   to follow Christ,
   to sing your song.
May we remember our fugue.
May we sing it in the way we live,
   in imitation of him.

Water into Wine

*L*ord, there are times when a new work is
   presented that is totally unsingable.
We think to ourselves,
"What could the composer be thinking?"
Surely no one would do this on purpose.

When we return to the work a week later,
   something miraculous has happened.
The composer sneaked back and changed the music.
It sounds pretty good.
The disjointed parts are melding
   into a haunting harmony.
The flat taste of water has become
   the robust body of the good wine.
This music is beautiful.

Lord, renew our trust in you.
Often you hand us a situation
   that seems impossible ...
   a financial crisis,
   a death,
   a stumbling child,
   a difficult relationship,
   an unresolved illness ...
   times when we are asked to wait

for your answer and help ...
times when we are to wait for good wine.

Let our music teach us this lesson, Lord.
Let us believe in your will in our lives.
We want to let you pick the music of our days.
We'll learn to sing it.
And someday appreciate the wisdom
    of your choice.

Priming the Pump

*L*ord, why is beginning so hard?
　　Remember when we stood poised to sing
　　that hymn we knew so well.
The first note came forth
　　like the long awaited first drop from the
　　ketchup bottle.
We sounded like the roll of an old engine
　　that won't turn over.
Then, after languishing for quite some time,
　　we decided to move on to the second note.
We spent the first six measures being pulled
　　by our director.
Mid-hymn we were up to tempo.
But priming a rusty old pump
　　would have been easier.

Lord, slow starts plague us all,
　　not only in the way we sing
　　but in the way we live.
There are times when our spirits drag,
　　when life goes into slow motion.
We can't get excited about a thing.
Lord, tonight we pray for the energy to give
　　every moment, every tempo,
　　the truth it deserves,
　　even when we don't feel like it.

Help us to recognize when we are slowing
    down.
Give us the discipline to speed up,
    whether it's procrastinating our way out
    of a difficult chore,
    or singing a dirge when *allegro* is called for.
Prime our pumps, Lord.

Love Songs

*L*ord, love songs are the easiest songs to
   sing.
They are sung when words alone fail,
     sung when the spirit breaks from its hiding
     place, to touch the spirit of another.
Love songs are written in moments
     of pure spirit,
     when we lose the confines of our physical
     state
     and fly to a loftier place,
     and there,
     in that place,
     sweet love is celebrated.

Lord, singing a love song to you
     is called a hymn.
In its beginning the hymn
     was conceived in pure spiritual love.
Sung first by one who had met and loved you.
Then, commanded by you,
     the singer shares the song
     so that others might also love.
But the song changes,
     as it passes through generations,
     through churches,

through believers and unbelievers,
     that sweet hymn loses its power.
All that remains is an empty token
     of a remembered love.
Lord, we have volumes of songs,
     volumes of hymns,
     that lie like dry bones
     waiting for your breath.
Make life and inspired love vibrate
     through these hymns again.
Call us back into the origins of these hymns.
Let us sing them as if we are the first singers
     of the love songs,
     and you the welcome listener.

Fifty Calories an Hour!

*L*ord, it is said that we burn fifty calories
   an hour singing.
In a two-hour rehearsal a choir of forty
   has expended four thousand calories.
This is an unexpected bonus for our service.
Yet you say that our gift of service
   should be given without expecting return,
   given freely because you have
   given so freely.
However, you are too generous a Lord.
Your track record is outstanding.
A boy gives five fishes;
   you feed hundreds with leftovers:
   gourmet wine at a country wedding on you,
   an encore for Lazarus,
   a prison break for Peter.
You love to surprise those
   who give to you without reserve.
Surprise them with unexpected wonder,
   the way fathers do.
So thank you, Lord, for spent calories.
And may we add that working for you
   is a pleasure.
Your benefit plan is wonderful,
   unorthodox,
   but wonderful.

Many but One

*L*ord, you know that choral singing is not
easy.
The fragile melding of sound that produces
the perfect balance of harmony
does not just happen.
It is the product of a willful choice to give up
one's own sound identity ...
No longer many individuals
singing the same notes,
but the marvelous wonder of the larger,
united voice of many.
The sound is rich in depth, many colored,
yet as singular as a drop of rain.
It is called blending ...
only the finest choirs achieve it.

Blending means forgetting about one's need
to be heard.
It means working in a selfless way
for the greater good.
It comes only when we can lose ourselves
in the creative movement of the music.

Many parts are gathered into the sound
of one body in prayer song.

Not an easy task, Lord!
Yet, the call isn't new.
Life is full of blending moments.
Discipleship demands it.
Living as Jesus did means
    giving up our own need for love of another,
    parents sacrificing for the good of a child,
    listening to the sufferings of another,
    serving a meal at a soup kitchen.
These too are another form of blending.
Living together in Christ requires this
    blending,
    whether in this music place
    or in our everyday world.
We are called to lay down our lives
    for one another.
Lord, give us the grace to blend.
May the choice to lose our own voice
    in this choir
    be a simple sign for you
    that we understand what you ask of us.
We understand the call to community,
    whether it is in song or in life.

What a Wonderful Gift!

*L*ord, how easy it is to take for granted
the power of the gift of song.
We have become very accustomed to
our spiritual sound ...
the crowded church ...
the spirit in our midst.
Yet every so often it is good
to set ourselves apart
and think about worship without music.
Then we can see the grace and power of
your gift.
What if there were only words for prayer,
and never that fine sweet melody
that transforms a quiet hope
into a triumphant Alleluia?
What if asking for mercy could only be
spoken?
What if we could never laugh
and sing the Gloria?

Music is the only way
your people can get beyond themselves
and touch heaven.
Music is a divine vehicle and
extraordinary grace

that allows us to clap our hands
together with you.
You lift us to the place
where our spirits can dance,
free of earth,
free of death,
free of every bond.

Lord, keep us mindful
that we are ministers of the finest grace.
Help us to remember that,
without your spirit song
which you sing through us,
many would never feel your touch,
many would forget your words of love.
You honor us with a gift beyond measure.
With your help, may we treasure it.

New Wine

*L*ord, how wonderfully we are made.
How often have we put aside a difficult
   work,
   only to pick it up again
   and sing it very well.
Something happened within.
The music rested in our minds.
And when we brought it forth again,
   it was infinitely better,
   as if you changed it in the silence.
Our minds did not forget.
They matured and aged the music,
   like a rare, sweet wine.
Could it be that as the song slept within us,
   you were at work?
Did the Spirit of wisdom and grace,
   the singer of the Pentecost song,
   take our music,
   polish and perfect it
   and return it to us
   in the night of our silence?
No longer rough,
   but smooth and fine.
Do you inspire in the unknown places
   of our minds?

Do we see that the Spirit is a singer too,
    complementing,
    bringing understanding,
    enriching,
    still creating among us,
    taking our unmade songs—grapes of
    promise—
    and turning them into wine?

Sweet and gentle Lord,
    we thank you for the gift of your Spirit.

A Place in the Choir

"All God's creatures got a place in the
choir.
Some sing lower.
Some sing higher.
Some sing out loud on a telephone wire
And some just clap their hands …
    or paws …
    or anything they got."

Lord, these words, taken from a
    children's hymn,
    express what we are all about.
We open the gate to everyone.
The choir isn't a place for the elite,
    the accomplished singer,
    the polished professional,
    even though they are also welcome.
The choir is kind of like heaven,
    where getting in is a matter of love.

Lord, so often we get carried away with
    ourselves,
    and others, who observe us,
    think they could never sing
    so as to deserve a place in this choir.

But you know differently,
    you the Creator who turned dew into
    manna,
    water into wine,
    clay into finest pottery.
You have a space for every voice.
Keep us humble in our task,
    humble enough to know that every voice,
    no matter how weak or strong,
    is beautiful and has a place here.
For to you, each of our voices sounds
    wonderful.
Whether we "sing out loud on a
    telephone wire,
    or just clap our hands ... or paws ...
    or anything we got."

Twice Blessed!

*L*ord, what are we doing here?
 We are so varied in our backgrounds ...
   office workers and mechanics,
   widows and high school students,
   secretaries and businessmen.

Yet, Lord, when we come together in this
     place,
   all our titles are dropped.
We become lovers of song and singers of
   praise.

We have learned a secret.
No matter where we spend our day,
   no matter what our gifts,
   music enhances and enriches it all.

The songs we learn here—return to us in the
     midst of a tedious afternoon.
They sing through our hearts and minds
   when our hands are involved
   in the business of the day,
   and we enjoy a retreat,
   a moment of beauty in the mundane.

We are learning what the psalmist David
  knew:
    musical prayer edifies the spirit,
    keeps us in touch with the Holy Spirit
    who sings to us when we least expect it.
    So it is that we are twice blessed.
We have the honor to offer song in worship.
We are honored as the song is returned to us
  in the quiet moments of our daily lives.

Thank you, Lord.
Amen.

The Master's Hand

*L*ord, our tempos and your tempos are not
always the same.
Sometimes you change the signatures of
our lives, and we don't even notice.

In a choir every eye must be trained
on the director.
It is the hand of the director which
determines the tempo.
When even one singer is unaware
of the musical pace,
disaster looms ... confusion mounts ...
crystal clear song becomes muddy water.

When our eyes stray from your hands, O Lord,
our lives become as muddied as our song.
But being sensitive to your hands
takes diligence, commitment, trust.
It takes a desire of the heart to offer our will
to another.
In music the results are immediate and
beautiful.
An alert choir produces a clarity of sound
that bespeaks dedication to its ministry.

However, the effect in our life with you
    is more subtle.
Keeping pace with you produces a peace and
    a deep sense of well-being.
Lord, teach us these two lessons well.
May the simple task of keeping
    the director's tempo
    lead us to the greater task of
    following your directions in our lives.
Help us to see that a simple example
    is to be found in our musical skill,
    an example that will lead us
    to a deeper understanding
    of how you direct our lives.

Just as we sing,
    so, too, should we follow you.

That Gospel Sound

*L*ord, some people can sing gospel,
  and some can't.
Some of your singers have that gospel sound
  in their very souls.
Their music is unwritten and heartfelt.
When they sing, their whole bodies
  move with the beat.
Their praise is such a "joyful noise"
  that they dance their praise.
Good gospel music makes our feet tap
  and our hands clap.

There are whole communities of the faithful
  who fill their worship with this sound,
  and the rest of God's people are edified
  by its beauty.

There are also others who look at gospel music
  in a printed score and, try as they may,
  never quite get there musically.
While gospel is meant to make a choir
  "sing like eagles,"
  some folks sing it like waddling ducks.

Lord, help us remember
    that there are many gifts
    and many singers in your kingdom.
Not everyone can sing every style of music,
    nor do they need to.
Each musical style offers
    a new way to praise you,
    a new way to reflect your love,
    a new way to inspire one another.

Lord, thank you for the many splendored array
    of song.
Thank you for gospel and jazz
    and folk and classical.
Thank you for one another.

Well Done, Good and Faithful Servant

*L*ord, singing with confidence
    takes a lot of courage.
A good choir is composed of individuals
    who choose to blend their voices
    into one sound ...
    but, if asked, could sing their part alone
    and with certainty.

But, Lord, just as in our lives, the ideal is not
        the reality.
Our choir has but relatively few people
    who have that confidence.
The rest of us need the support
    of strong voices
    to keep us on track.
We would rather come to church in our
    pajamas
    than sing alone.

Yet, Lord, you expect us to keep growing.
And in music this means not being
    comfortable
    leaning on the skills of others.
It means pushing ourselves to sing well and
    independently.

The choir provides an arena for one of life's
    simple lessons.
Your vision of us is grander than we could
    ever suppose.
You keep asking us to reach beyond ourselves,
    to keep growing till we have exhausted life,
    till we fly into your eternal life.
Each step forward enhances the treasure
    we are.
When we do nothing, our beauty is
    diminished.

Lord, keep us reaching, growing,
    expanding the talent you have given us.
May we be like the servant
    who doubled the talents received,
    so that you may say to us,
"Well done, good and faithful servant."

Elusive Pitch

*L*ord, give us the gift of accurate pitch.
Pitch is the subtle difference that marks a fine,
    polished choir.
It separates those who are disciplined
    about their gift
    from those who work more casually.
Pitch calls us to sing with sensitive ears,
    poised for the slightest hint
    of flattening or sharpening.
Hearing well is as important as singing well.
Each sense supports the other.
We learn to hear ourselves.
We listen humbly,
    never too proud to believe that our voices
    could be faulted.
Just as our walk with you is a constant vigil
    to keep in loving grace,
    so too is there a vigil of sound in our choir.
In a way, being off key is a lot like sin.
It can happen when we let our guard down,
    when we think we're beyond failure.

Lord, keep us humble enough to know that
    even simple skills take constant work.
Thank you for giving us ears to hear our music
    as others hear it.

Bless our voices and our ears
　　that they might work
　　as companions in song.
One is no more important than the other.
Good pitch is a grace.
Lord, we ask that you pour forth this simple
　　grace on our musical offering.

Smile!

*L*ord, some of the best musical advice
   we can ever receive is
   "Before you begin to sing ...
   take a deep breath ...
   and smile!"

A momentary pause and then a smile
   cleanse the spirit of all tension.
Smiling lets our spirits remember
   the joy of our song.
Making ourselves smile,
   even when we don't feel like smiling,
   changes the musical mood.
And the song more free
   unleashes a spiritual sparkle
   that comes from the Spirit within us.

In that release of tension
   we let go of all our concern for the song
   and your gift and grace take over.
The lesson is one of life's simplest.
Sometimes acting "as if" lets it happen.
It is as if we trust you
   in what will happen with our song.
We believe you will sustain our effort.

When we have done our best
    to prepare the music,
    when our work is done,
    we release the music into your hands,
    with trust, love, and with a smile.

Receive this smiling choir, Lord.
Our smiles speak of our trust in you.
You teach us the ways of faith and of song.
You teach us to sing with a joyful smile.
O Lord, for this we praise and thank you.

A People of Praise

*L*ord, a choir director once said,
"At this morning's performance ..."
Whether he knew it or not,
    he thought of the music ministry's role
    as performing rather than praising.
O Lord, what a dangerous difference.
The moment a choir forgets what it is about,
    the moment we start worshiping ourselves
    and our sound,
    instead of you,
    at that moment we lose our power
    to serve the body of Christ.
We lose the ability to fill your house
    with authentic praise.
We lose our call as ministers of song.
We become frivolous ornaments,
    shadows of what we are to be.

Keep us mindful of our calling.
Keep our hearts and minds
    in a posture of service.
May we never presume that those gathered
    have come for our benefit,
    but always to worship you.

Keep our music fitting to that worship
    so that our song will never outshine
    the ritual itself.
Let our song enhance and enliven
    your sacred rite.
Lord, if we have failed to do this in the past,
    we ask your forgiveness.
We mean to sing for you alone.
Amen.

Ending the Year

Magnificat

Lord, these final weeks of singing always
    seem to be the most difficult.
While singing the well-mastered hymns,
    and resting in the after-Pentecost days,
    there is little to get excited about.
The spirit of the church is quieting into a
    peace.
The Alleluias are fading.
Earth life itself settles into a piano of
    temperate green.

Yet, even though our inspiration wanes,
    you remain with us in these days.
You never lack for attention or love of us.
You hear the hymns of May
    with the same delight
    as the poignant sweet melodies of
    Christmas.
In fact, what means more to you
    is the quiet faithful song,
    not the occasional shining moment.
We spend most of our lives doing simple,
    unnoticed, tedious tasks.
And you love us for it.
Mary, the lady of this month,
    spent most of her life in obscurity,
    living the ways of a poor Jewish woman.

She sang only one song . . .
Magnificat.
Then she spent a lifetime living her song,
   unnoticed.
Lord, help us to remember her courageous
   example.
Even in life's quieter times,
   may we be content with our song.
When no one notices or cares,
   let us remember that singers become saints
   in quiet service.

In Praise of Autumn

*L*ord, autumn is beginning,
   and as singers it is important
    to soak up your display.
Keep our souls in touch with your hand
    in the natural life around us.
We are the vessels of musical poetry,
    a poetry that cannot be sung if the vessel
    has forgotten to marvel at the poet.
So tonight we share a moment
    of autumn marvel,
    to keep us always wondering,
    always in awe,
    always in praise of you, the poet.

We praise you for the brush of orange
    on the trees
    reminding us that life comes full circle
    for each of us.
We praise you for cool nights
    giving rest to our weariness.
We praise you for the sweet smell of harvest
    reassuring us of your good providence.
We praise you for the changing air,
    whose cold wind teaches us to find
    inner warmth in your love.

We praise you for the light frost on the
    morning grass
    telling us to see beauty in even a small
    misfortune.
We praise you for the laughter of children
    playing in leaves,
    for it warns us not to let the magic
    pass us by.
For all these things we give thanks and praise.
For you, our marvelous poet,
    never fail to amaze us
    with your gifts,
    autumn gifts,
    which help our music come so easily.

The Voice of God

Lord, new colors begin to grace the earth.
Autumn begins in a whisper of yellow,
   only to explode into the vibrant reds
   of October.
The air is subtly hinting of things to come.
It is time to quiet our hearts,
   to hear your voice.
We are called to a quieting,
   a peace apart.

Such a quiet seems to contradict our nature
   as music makers.
We delight in making a "joyful noise."
Lord, teach us to reverence the quiet,
   to whisper our song
   when the music calls us.
The gentle psalm sung to a silent heart
   bespeaks the voice of God.
We become your voice
   to the heart of our listener.
Keep us sensitive to that call.
Give us the grace to seek out a quiet sound.
Your voice is a humble one,
   heard by those who wait in the quiet.

May our music serve you, Lord,
    singing in the hush
    your word
    to a people
    who can easily forget
    the quiet voice of God
    in a noisy, confusing world.

Giving Thanks

*L*ord, this is the time of year
for giving thanks.
We have so much to thank you for.

Thank you for the profound gift of inspiration
   that accompanies our music.
Thank you for sustaining the quality
   of our sound.
Thank you for ears that are becoming sensitive
   to pitch.
Thank you for the ability to laugh at ourselves.
Thank you for new music, always bringing a
   challenge to our skills.
Thank you for the faithfulness of our members,
   for people who sing with enthusiasm,
   for high notes and low notes,
   and especially, for one another.